earth
ignored
your cries

c p beauvoir

ISBN: 978-0-9975066-4-8 (Paperback)
ISBN: 978-0-9975066-5-5 (E-book)
ISBN: 978-0-9975066-6-2 (Audiobook)
ISBN: 978-0-9975066-7-9 (Audiobook)

Library of Congress Control Number: 2019907944

Leef Publishing LLC
151 N Nob Hill Road
Suite 388
Plantation, FL 33324

Printed in the United States of America

Written by C P Beauvoir
Edited by Brenda Peregrine
Illustrations by Rodney Sanon
Cover Design and Formatting by Damonza

cpbeauvoir.com
leefpublishing.com

also by c p beauvoir

things left unsaid

for
maurice sixto

contents

earth and her mind

sweat and tears and screams
through pain and blood life is born
empowered by love

seeds of misery
shamefully grow wounded plants
bearing fruits of pain

of black witch with wings
and white sorceress with corns
bright light shines within

broken hearts and souls
tell their secrets to the dark
hoping light will hear

oppressed child of mine
chains and shackles don't enslave
those who free their minds

souls of light and love
inspire wounded hearts to heal
without persuasion

broken promises
breath balance serenity
heart to heart we are

shapeless borders swing
in the winds of heedless wounds
searching for freedom

bliss enthralled her heart
taking the first step of faith
from darkness to light

in the dark of night
oppressed voices sing loudly
free free free freedom

maybe it was you
the long lost love you searched for
was you all along

and who made you queen
of withholding forgiveness
from those who need it

darkness in your eyes
birthed from a lifetime of pain
only love can heal

rain and thunder poured
throughout the night as we held
each other tightly

step into the light
away from grumpy shadows
bloom as flowers do

the answers you seek
are not in them but in you
look inside yourself

—

look in the mirror
your greatest love is staring
saying *i love you*

hunched shoulders crawling
in the mud bruised and bloody
who will wash your wounds

tainted traitor's blood
wicked veins full of envy
hatred is your name

children of the sun
smile through bruised skin broken backs
as their children die

breath moved through her chest
like the ripples of rivers
flowing peacefully

there are no answers
to truly explain why you
were violated

uplifted by love
supported by life lessons
moving me forward

love painted colors
of red and purple sunsets
forming arts of hearts

love opened my heart
like the bud of an orchid
slowly steadily

see yourself in truth
with eyes of love and passion
nothing else will do

love protected me
in ways unknown to my mind
but felt by my heart

25

there's a storm coming
battle of rain and thunder
over air and earth

can a butterfly
fly from flower to flower
without pretty wings

drowning in the pool
of fear pain and misery
waiting to be saved

the flower of life
created nectars of love
feeding light to heart

darling close your eyes
feel the beatings of our hearts
our song is playing

the bells are ringing
shut the doors close the windows
the devils are here

the fool and the wise
dance in the rain together
crying happy tears

who dare convince you
that the *less than* illusion
is in fact real

loving all of me
left no place for doubt or fear
to live in my heart

draw me close to you
kiss my wounds caress my fears
hold me in your arms

time waits for no one
no regards for goals or dreams
without you it goes

imprinted in love
energy calls me daughter
light named me first born

—

set the atmosphere
to the aroma of love
and the scent of peace

the light within you
shielded you from the darkness
shadowing your soul

stripped to skin and bones
lashes cutting like a knife
earth ignored your cries

my heart longs for you
with the same intensity
darkness longs for light

born in a river
ripples of battles and wars
and the peace to come

see with eyes of truth
hear with ears of compassion
speak with words of love

—

on the other side
of the many things you fear
your dreams are waiting

—

step out of ego
dive into your loving heart
where your true home is

clouds drifted away
an empty blue sky grieving
their prompt return home

no sanctuary
in a mind born of judgment
a heart full of hate

intertwined by love
sealed by the promise of us
two bodies one soul

come into my heart
to a loving paradise
our heaven to share

vicious hurricanes
bringing the wrath of the seas
with winds of fury

wash me with your touch
bathe me in the tenderness
of the love we share

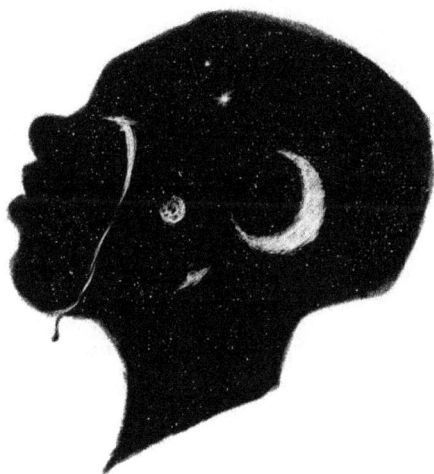

cry no more my child
the universe heard your cries
healing is coming

dwell with me in love
take my hands kiss my fingers
i am yours to have

i often wonder
if there was ever a time
humans were at peace

—

when the world was new
love flavored the atmosphere
then the humans came

a group of ten ants
one vision one mission rule
a thousand lions

a reality
life of better days and nights
for the afflicted

strange bleeding creatures
broken bodies wreck the earth
souls long dead and gone

your scars are roadmaps
a journey of survival
the healing you found

when everyone leaves
empty thoughts invade your mind
fill your heart with love

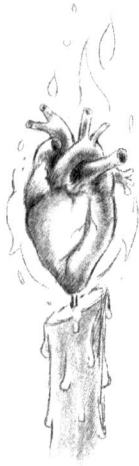

when the lights go out
and darkness swallows the world
your heart is the light

bones beneath the earth
praying to the rocks below
to save them from dust

the children of god
preach peace and brotherly love
kill children of men

heal at your own pace
step by step day after day
again and again

watching our men die
the never ending bloodshed
infants on our backs

look inside my heart
see my bleeding wounds and scars
love me with my faults

you are not alone
the universe is with you
in all that you do

—

unconditional
love for self is your birthright
destined legacy

—

the pillars of life
stand on rocks of acceptance
rooted in true love

—

the deliverance
of your heart must come from you
as act of self love

pastors of the church
preaching the gospel of christ
between children's legs

earth and her heart

the juices of me
rouse the garden of your mouth
let your thirst be quenched

sweet kisses of love
our lips locked a thousand times
since the start of us

cut your heart open
place it in my greedy hands
unworthy of love

the wheel of patience
spins the atmosphere of earth
through the end of times

the promise of hope
the belief of better days
for the afflicted

the fountain of love
created in the heavens
flows inside your heart

and when darkness comes
waging bloody war on soul
light is your savior

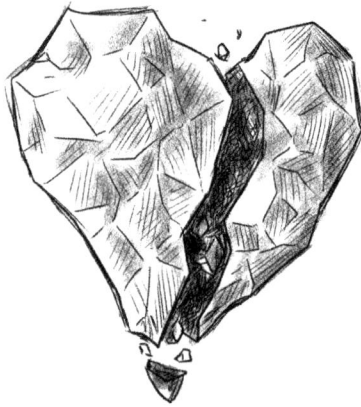

broken hearts crying
begging those who wounded them
to love them again

immortals planning
ruin of eternity
in the world of men

small beacon of hope
radiates the brightest flame
in the darkest hearts

legacies are built
through hard work and sacrifice
by the men who care

the present moment
not of the past or future
the here and the now

i am yours to have
through trials tribulations
sweet love of my heart

the portal of life
the path to heaven and hell
is paved in our hearts

he who speaks the truth
to self in dangerous times
the son of wisdom

blue seas of freedom
mountains of aspirations
the heaven of dreams

respect the planet
every path on mother earth
leads us to ourselves

the dusk light of earth
illuminates the night sky
lovers of blackness

the journey inward
the road of discovery
the pathway to self

the one i wanted
was not the one i needed
to show me the way

angels surround me
the universe blesses me
each and every day

every obstacle
that crumbled me to the ground
taught me a lesson

oh how i love you
universe sweet universe
my home in all homes

sugar sweet sugar
lick the salt from my body
make me your honey

fatherless daughters
begging the presence of men
they have never met

the birds are singing
the flowers are opening
the sun has risen

my manhood is yours
open your mouth my darling
take me inside you

the bondage of men
not of body but of mind
destruction of lives

women of the earth
singing the praises of men
who murdered their souls

sons of broken men
ashamed of the tears they cry
and their wounded hearts

the world is changing
destruction of human life
the absence of love

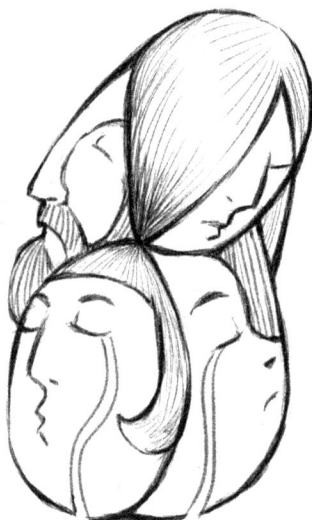

mothers and fathers
weeping for their dead children
no one hears their cries

to be around you
priceless and cherished treasure
the gift of my heart

the burning of souls
who have yet to see the light
in the flames of hell

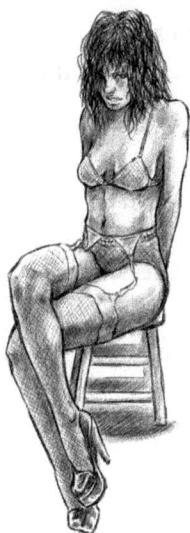

sensations of lust
buried between women's legs
the sixth sense of men

stay with me my love
through the light and the darkness
of this strange wild world

—

pleasures of bodies
sacred bonding of our hearts
the triumph of souls

—

i treasure your heart
respect and adore your mind
i cherish your soul

the love of our hearts
infinite roads and valleys
eternal forests

angels of heaven
whisper the secrets of love
to demons of hell

the sun and the stars
conspire against planet earth
our mother is scared

betrayal of soul
battle of mind war of heart
weapons of self harm

corners of the rooms
without walls and foundations
longing for the cage

the air smelled of grief
blood watered the frozen earth
of winter flowers

divine are the souls
creating their own heaven
from the gates of hell

bodies entangled
in the bed of loneliness
and sheets of regret

sun withheld his light
darkness claimed the galaxy
earth cried to the moon

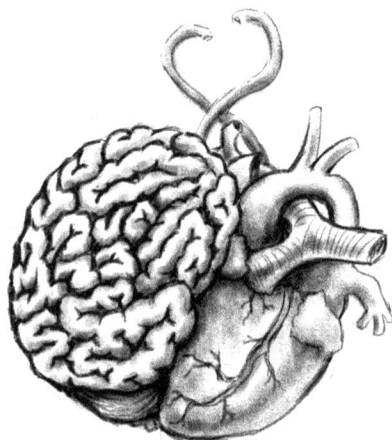

conditions of love
manipulation of minds
control lonely hearts

the carving of earth
the enrichment of the few
above the many

betrayal of vows
broken trust loss of respect
the death of marriage

the pit of despair
lives in the lovely bodies
of the troubled hearts

shadow of the sun
bonded to the light of day
through heaven and hell

—

of gold and diamonds
wealth sublimated beneath
the rags of the poor

the lone star of hope
lives in the vast emptiness
of a thousand hearts

steer your wildest dream
through the winds of doubt and fear
the storm of terror

under the weather
blue skies poured rain red as blood
dirt rose in the air

denial of truth
static field of illusion
sprinting past the lies

old eyes stare at you
ancient souls from distant worlds
trust your ancestors

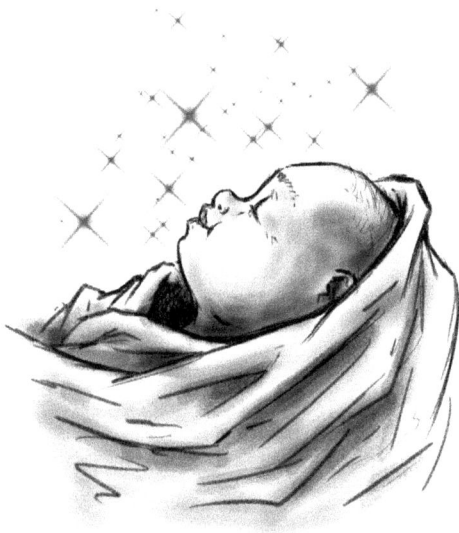

how magnificent
is the smile of a newborn
melting monsters' hearts

the chameleon
who wished death on the rainbow
envied her colors

what your mind accepts
when not aligned with your heart
will trouble your soul

seven billion souls
worshiped the presence of you
still you were lonely

your friends are strangers
warm bodies friendly faces
trusted murderers

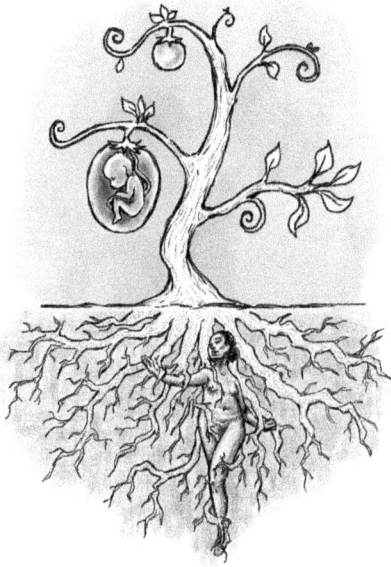

i planted the seed
your womb nurtures the harvest
don't murder our fruit

the colors of earth
are painted on black bodies
called inferior

the fabric of time
woven through uncertainty
seal the aloof past

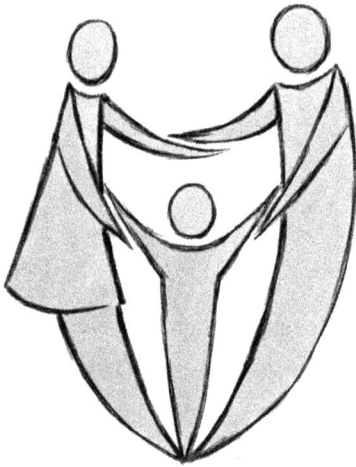

society said
she was a foreign system
controlling our minds

and i've come to see
society is us men
women and children

when will adults learn
truth falls from the mouths of babes
young bodies wise minds

rotten are the minds
ancient bodies walking earth
who have learned nothing

respected elders
are not of age nor of time
but of lessons learned

who protects the men
used and abused by women
with the wicked hearts

what a tragedy
to have conquered everything
yet gifted nothing

life loves me today
more than it did yesterday
less than tomorrow

a justice system
built for the liberation
of the powerful

the prisons were built
for the children of the slaves
who dare seek freedom

armor of justice
forged in the fires of truth
steel of bravery

the innocent die
fighting the wars of the men
who have never bled

under the rainbow
mountains rise beneath the dirt
claiming the heavens

warm oven baked bread
fingers digging in the crust
joy waters my mouth

bagel and cream cheese
along with hot chocolate
breakfast of lovers

strawberry keeps on
falling in love with mango
such passionate fruits

the gods are at war
worlds are dying everywhere
heaven is no more

the battle for souls
waged without murder weapons
but with joyful toys

world war three is fought
not for country or duty
but for hearts and minds

tell me how you felt
setting fire to their homes
as you claimed their land

cut their throats open
pierce the daggers through their hearts
kill them kill them all

the babies went up
grey machetes became red
piercing their bellies

to destroy a man
rob him of his wife and child
his reasons for life

the tears of a man
burst from his eyes abruptly
when his heart explodes

to win a man's heart
navigate his deepest fears
and map out his strengths

let us thank the men
paving the roads of freedom
and the path of dreams

protector of life
provider of treasured home
our trusted leader

earth and her soul

red river of moon
flows between a woman's legs
enticing her mood

pain and pleasure come
during the time of the month
the moon speaks your name

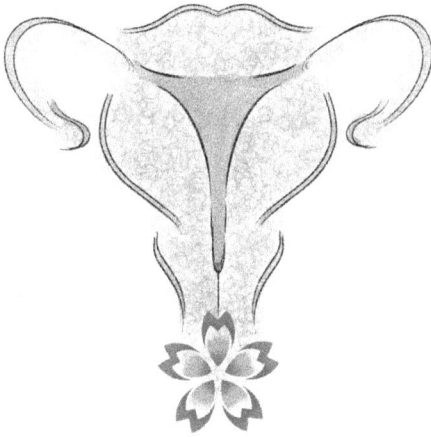

precious ovaries
blessed are fallopian tubes
where egg and sperm meet

a woman's body
is the beauty of nature
the blessing of earth

an act of courage
carrying life in your womb
in this deadly world

divine are women
who sacrifice their bodies
for the innocent

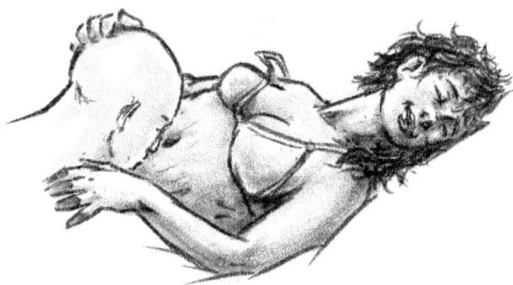

make love to my skin
kiss the scars and marks of birth
as though they're my lips

the goddess of love
is the nurturer of life
the queen of mankind

love a woman's soul
pleasure the depths of her mind
before her body

how brave is the love
of a woman completely
in love with herself

an honest woman
rarest exquisite creature
one in a million

we are all equal
both men and women are the
creations of god

joy love and respect
for all the roles and functions
that brighten our souls

speak of period
of humanity on earth
hell paved paradise

the city of saints
built with the blood of sinners
on the bricks of hell

the blood has been washed
cleansed of the impurities
poisoning our hearts

lovers don't forget
the hateful songs the heart sings
when it is angry

show me a true heart
with the bruises and the scars
that has healed itself

blurry souls asking
devils of eternal hell
a seat in heaven

the world of phony
envy the authentic hearts
who don't wear a mask

people will hang you
for speaking the very truth
they see with their eyes

i knew you lost me
the moment you wished and prayed
i was someone else

—

now that i love me
i remain faithful and true
to me and myself

how can i thank you
you saw everything in me
when i saw nothing

you picked up the load
crumbling my knees on the floor
so i could stand up

the heavens bless us
for accepting each other
with all of our scars

paradise is you
wrapping your arms around me
when i feel alone

nipples getting hard
fingers sliding inside me
your lips on my breasts

suck the lovely dots
planted on my breasts like the
sweet candies you love

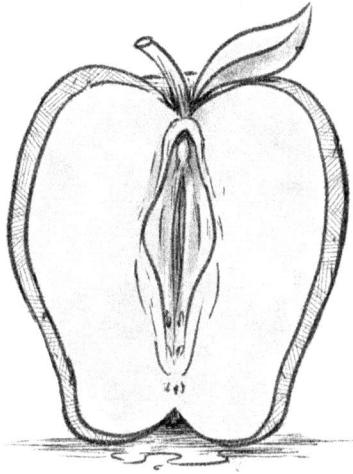

the circumference
your soft lips slide all around
the sweetness of me

your tongue slides in me
slowly licking the honey
dripping down my legs

—

my favorite ride
is taken on your manhood
on top of our bed

you taste like power
sprinkled with sugar and salt
the most fun flavors

glorious body
art of masculinity
the kingdom of love

body to body
making love under the stars
lover to lover

the marriage of hearts
who love without conditions
last eternally

truth begins with you
stating your expectations
without fear or shame

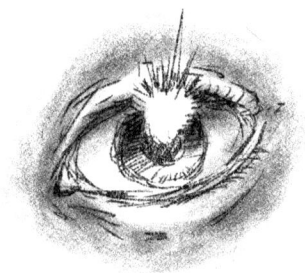

amongst all the stars
you remain the brightest light
shining for my heart

self acceptance asked
that i receive myself with
the good and the bad

a good cry can heal
any pain any trouble
burdening your soul

thunders smacking air
lightning burning the ether
violence on earth

the rain's cries are clear
absent the lovely colors
healing rainbow's heart

earth rotates the sun
hoping he chooses her love
above that of moon

—

moon reflects sun's light
and shows off to the planets
jealous of their love

—

lovely moon of mine
bathe in the light and the warmth
my sun's rays are yours

she who lights the sparks
of the honeymoon of self
oh what a woman

i stand before you
as i came into the world
take me as i am

did you hear the wind
singing to the leaves and dust
dancing in her breeze

loyal waves stay with
the ocean though tempted by
evaporation

growth resides beyond
metal barbed wires of safety
on the fields of doubt

the caterpillar
first came as an egg before
being butterfly

war lord in our rank
envision a world of peace
won through the bloodshed

scared minds and wise souls
say peace must be won with peace
but it never is

shall we pray or fight
for peace to remain supreme
on the lands we love

mother earth loves us
let us take a holy vow
love her in return

love yourself today
with all your imperfections
you deserve your love

speak of the secrets
weighing heavy on your heart
free your troubled soul

—

when you came to be
the creator birthed you here
worthy is your name

you are not your past
neither are you the future
you're the present time

i choose to see me
in love and in truth as my
creator sees me

—

life is not a dream
nor is it a nightmare from
which you can escape

—

here you are loving
yourself and everyone else
in spite of the pain

you deserve the world
the holy gifts of heaven
you shall have it all

you are so much more
than the restrictive labels
the world brands you with

you were meant to love
and be loved in return you
are worthy of love

stay in love with you
like the waves stay with the sea
and light stays with sun

there's joy in your heart
and light shining in your eyes
such warmth in your smile

you are magical
love's most beloved creature
i thank love for you

dreaming is the bridge
between what the heart can feel
and the mind can build

red and orange suns
blue skies green seas dancing with
fire and water

warm hugs sweet kisses
a glance across the hallway
love is in the air

stay with me tonight
let's create magic between
us from dusk to dawn

the story of us
our failures and victories
a tale worth telling

home is you and i
minds connecting hearts joining
souls rising in love

feel the love of god
living in and around you
so pure and so true

you are the image
of the divine creator
you are perfection

honey you are loved
by the earth and the sun and
the moon and the stars

your energy fuels
love and light in distant worlds
you have yet to see

wish the past goodbye
the future is unwritten
cheers to the new you

never be afraid
to let go and start over
breathe love exhale fear

you can't walk away
from the power of true love
true love lives in you

a moment alone
in silence brings clarity
sacred time with self

shift your perception
from victim to survivor
power lives in choice

speak the truth to light
you've been silent for too long
let earth hear you roar

i was introduced to haiku poems, a traditional japanese form of poetry, through andria thomas, my friend, and immediately fell in love with the three lines poem of five, seven, and five syllables; but the thing that captivated me the most was the ability to write powerful thoughts in a simple form.

i've always had thousands of thoughts swirling in my mind. and i have always felt they needed to be written down on paper but i also believed that these thoughts were too short to be written and published as a book.

i wrote my first haiku poem on saturday may 7, 2016 in honor of mother's day which was to be celebrated on the very next day, the second sunday of may in the united states.

after writing my first haiku poem, i felt as though i discovered a channel through which my thoughts could come alive on paper. and after writing hundreds of haiku poems, i felt strongly that it was time to share them with the world. this is how the *earths, suns, moons, and stars* book series started with *earth ignored your cries* as the first book in my collection of haiku poems.

i follow the lines and syllables rules to write my haiku poems but my haiku poems are not "traditional". they are simply haiku poems written from the depth of my heart to yours.

the art of writing belongs with me, not to me. we met and became lovers, intertwined through thousands of words both written and unwritten—an endless journey of love.

— c p beauvoir